Zac's Train Ride

MW01122442

Story by Jackie Tidey
Photography by Lindsay Edwards

Zac and Mum and Dad
went to see
the Puffing Billy train.

"Look at the big boys and girls,"
said Zac.

"They are going for a ride
on Puffing Billy," said Mum.

"Can I go for a ride, too?"
said Zac.

The girls and boys
got on the train.

"My wheelchair is too big
to go on the train," said Zac.
"I can not go for a ride."

"Mum will get a man
to help us," said Dad.

Mum came back.

"Can I get on the train?"
said Zac.

"Yes," said Mum.
"A man is coming
to help us."

"Here comes the man," said Mum.

The man said to Zac,
"You can go on the train."

The man got a big ramp.

"Here we go!" said Zac.